The Adventures of
Thor the Mighty
In the Land of the Giants

© Translated by Bernard Scudder

Illustrations: Gunnar Karlsson
Editor: Jón Þórisson
Cover design and layout: Helgi Hilmarsson

© GUDRUN 2007, Reykjavík

ISBN 9979-787-37-6
ISBN 978-9979-78-737-2

Printed in India

The Adventures of
Thor the Mighty
In the Land of the Giants

Snorri Sturluson

Illustrated by Gunnar Karlsson

GUDRUN

1. Thor makes a feast with his goats

This tale begins when Thor set off with his goats and chariot, and the god named Loki went with him. In the evening they arrived at a farmer's house and were given lodging there for the night. That evening, Thor took both his goats and slaughtered them, then had them skinned and put in a cauldron. When they were cooked, Thor and his companion sat down to dinner. Thor invited the farmer and his wife and children to join them. The farmer's son was called Thjalfi and his daughter Roskva. Thor put the goat skins down away from the fire and told the farmer and his family to throw the bones onto them. Thjalfi, the farmer's son, held a goat's thigh-bone and split it with his knife to break it down to the marrow.

  Thor stayed there for the night. Just before dawn he got up and dressed, then took his hammer Mjöllnir and blessed the goat skins. The goats stood up again, but one had a lame hind leg. Noticing this, Thor thought that the farmer or someone in his family surely hadn't treated the goats' bones carefully. He could tell that the thigh-bone was broken.

2. Thor takes Thjalfi and Roskva into his service

There's no need to make a long story of it: everyone can tell how scared the farmer must have been when he saw the way Thor lowered his eyebrows over his eyes. But when he saw the look in Thor's eyes, he thought the sight alone would be enough to kill him. Thor gripped the shaft of his hammer so hard that his knuckles went white. The farmer and his family, naturally enough, cried out and begged for mercy, and offered to repay him with everything they owned.

When Thor saw how frightened they were his fury wore off and he calmed down. By way of settlement he took their children, Thjalfi and Roskva, and forced them to be his servants. They have always followed him ever since.

He left the goats behind there and started his journey eastwards to Giantland, all the way to the sea, and then he set out across the deep ocean. When he reached land he went ashore and Loki, Thjalfi and Roskva went with him.

3. At the Giant-King's gate

Thor and his companions went on their way and kept on walking until midday. Then they saw a fortress standing on a plain, so high that they had to throw their heads right back before they could see up to the top. They went up to the fortress and there was a gate across the entrance, which was closed. Thor tackled the gate but could not manage to open it. When they made a special effort to enter the fortress, they managed to get in by squeezing themselves through between the bars. They saw a huge hall and walked over to it. The door was open. They went inside and saw a lot of men, most of them very large, sitting on two benches. After that they went up to the king, Utgarda-Loki, and greeted him. But he took his time before he looked at them, then grinned and said:

"News travels slowly when the way is far. Or am I far off the mark in thinking that this little lad is Thor the Traveller? Surely you must be greater than you look. What feats do you and your companions feel you are capable of? No one is allowed to stay with us here who is not better than other men at some kind of skill or accomplishment."

4. Thor and his companions compete with the men of the king's court. Loki's feat.

Loki, who had entered last, said, "I can perform a feat which I'm quite prepared to put to the test: that no one here is quicker at eating his food than I am."

Utgarda-Loki answered, "That's some feat if you can do it, so let it be put to the test then." He called down the bench to tell the man called Logi to step out onto the floor and try himself against Loki.

Then a trough was fetched in, carried to the floor of the hall, and filled with meat. Loki sat at one end and Logi at the other, and each of them ate as quickly as he could. When they met in the middle, Loki had eaten all the meat off the bones, but Logi had eaten all the meat and the bones with it and the trough too, and it seemed clear to everyone that Loki had lost the game.

5. Thjalfi runs a race

Then Utgarda-Loki asked what the young man could do. Thjalfi said he would try running a race against anyone Utgarda-Loki appointed. Utgarda-Loki said this was a good feat to try and that he would expect him to have an exceptional gift of speed to manage it, but quickly had it put to the test. Utgarda-Loki got up and went outside, where there was a good course to run across the level plain. Then Utgarda-Loki called over a lad by the name of Hugi and told him to run a race against Thjalfi. They ran the first course, and Hugi was far enough ahead of him to turn back to meet him after reaching the end.

Then Utgarda-Loki said, "You'll need to make more effort, Thjalfi, if you are to win the race. All the same, it's true that no man has ever come here who is swifter of foot."

They ran another course, and when Hugi reached the end and turned back, Thjalfi was still a good arrow-shot away.

Then Utgarda-Loki said, "I think Thjalfi is running well, but I don't believe he'll win the contest now. But that will be put to the test when they run the third race."

They ran another race, but by the time Hugi reached the end and turned back, Thjalfi had not made it half-way along the course.

Then everyone said the feat had been put fully to the test.

6. Drinking from a long horn

Then Utgarda-Loki asked Thor what feat he would like to show them, after all the great stories that people have made about his mighty deeds. Thor said he would like most of all to try a drinking contest. Utgarda-Loki said this could be arranged, went into the hall and called to his table-servant, telling him to fetch the horn that his men always drank forfeits from. The table-servant brought in the horn and handed it to Thor.

Then Utgarda-Loki said, "Anyone who can finish this horn in a single draught is regarded as a good drinker. Some people take two draughts to finish it. But no one is such a poor drinker that he can't finish it in three."

Thor looked at the horn and did not think it was very large, although it was rather long. He was very thirsty, so he started drinking with huge gulps, not expecting to have to go down a second time. But when his breath ran out and he tipped up the horn to see how the drink was going, he could hardly notice any difference in the level inside it.

7. Plenty to take

Then Utgarda-Loki said, "You've drunk well, but not too much. I wouldn't have believed anyone who had told me that the god Thor couldn't drink more than that. But I know you'll finish it in the second draught."

Without replying, Thor put the horn to his mouth and planned to take a bigger drink. He pitted himself against the horn for as long as his breath lasted, but he could still see that the point of the horn would not lift as high as he wished. And when he took the horn from his mouth and looked inside, the level seemed to have gone down less than the first time, although it was low enough now for the horn to be carried without spilling.

Then Utgarda-Loki said, "What are you up to, Thor? Aren't you saving more than you can handle in a single drink? If you plan on finishing the horn in the third drink, it looks to me as if this one will have to be the biggest one. But we won't call you as great a man as the gods do, if you can't put on a better showing in the other contests than the way I think this one will turn out."

Then Thor got angry, put the horn to his mouth, drank furiously and held out for as long as he could. He looked inside the horn, and if he'd ever made any impression on it when he drank, it was this time. Then he handed over the horn and did not want to drink more.

8. Thor lifts the king's cat

Then Utgarda-Loki said, "It's obvious that your strength is not as great as we thought. But do you want to try some other challenge? You're clearly not any use at this one."

Thor replied, "I can still put several feats to the test. But I'd have been surprised, back home with the gods, if such a drink had been called little. Anyway, what do you want to challenge me to now?"

Then Utgarda-Loki said, "The young lads around here do a fairly unremarkable thing, they pick up my cat from the ground. I'd never have proposed such a thing to the god Thor if I hadn't seen that you're much weaker than I thought."

After that a fairly big grey cat ran out onto floor of the hall. Thor went up to it and put his hand under the middle of its belly and lifted it up, but the cat kept arching its back as much as Thor raised his hand. When Thor stretched as high up as he could, the cat lifted one foot from the ground, but Thor could not win the contest.

9. The final trial of strength

Then Utgarda-Loki said, "This contest turned out as I expected. The cat is pretty big, but Thor is short and puny compared with the great men who are here with us."

Then Thor said, "You might call me puny, but let someone here come and wrestle with me then! Now I'm angry!"

Looking around the benches, Utgarda-Loki replied, "I can't see any man in here who wouldn't consider it a trivial task to wrestle with you." Then he said, "Let's see to start with. Call in my nanny Elli, Thor can wrestle with her if he wants. She's brought down men who haven't looked any weaker than Thor is."

Then an old woman walked into the hall. Utgarda-Loki said she should wrestle with the god Thor. There is not much to say about the outcome of the fight: the harder that Thor grappled with her, the firmer she stood. Then the old woman began trying to get a grip on him, and Thor lost his balance, and there was a mighty struggle that lasted for some time before Thor fell to one knee. Then Utgarda-Loki went over and told them to stop wrestling, saying that Thor would not need to challenge anyone else to a wrestling match in his hall. Night had fallen by this time. Utgarda-Loki showed Thor and his companions to their seats and they stayed there all night in good company.

10. Thor and his companions prepare to leave

In the morning, at dawn, Thor and his companions got up and dressed and were ready to leave. Utgarda-Loki came over and had the tables laid for them. There was no lack of good company, food and drink. When they had eaten, they turned to leave.

Utgarda-Loki followed them out and walked with them outside the fortress. As they parted, Utgarda-Loki spoke to Thor and asked him how he felt his journey had turned out, and whether he had ever met a more powerful man. Thor said he couldn't claim to have won much honour from his dealings with him. "I know that you'll call me a weakling, and I don't like that."

Then Utgarda-Loki said, "Now that you have left the fortress I shall tell you the truth, and if I live and have my way you'll never enter it again. And I know for certain that you'd never have been let inside in the first place if I'd known beforehand how much strength you have. You almost brought disaster upon us. I deceived you by magic, and you didn't realise."

11. The magical king reveals the truth

"It was like this with the challenges you took up with my men. The first was what Loki did. He was very hungry and ate quickly. But Logi was really wildfire, and he consumed the trough at the same time as the meat. When Thjalfi ran the race against the man called Hugi, that was really my thoughts, and Thjalfi couldn't be expected to match them for speed.

"When you drank from the horn and thought you were making slow progress, I know for certain that I'd never have believed such a marvel was possible. One end of the horn was out in the ocean, and you couldn't see it. But when you reach the sea, you will see how much of it has dried up after you drank from it." This is called the tide now.

And he went on, "I didn't think it was any less remarkable when you lifted up the cat, and to tell you the truth, everyone was terrified when they saw you lift one of its feet from the earth. Because that cat wasn't what it seemed to you: it was the Midgard Serpent that lies encircling all lands, yet it was hardly long enough to keep its head and tail on the earth, because you stretched so high that it almost touched the heavens.

"The wrestling match was a great wonder, too, when you stood up for so long and only fell to one knee when you grappled with Elli, for she was actually old age. Because there has never been anyone, nor ever will be, if he lives long enough to face old age, who will not be toppled by old age in the end.

"And now, the truth is that we shall part, and it will be better for both of us if you never come to see me again. I shall defend my fortress again with such magic or other tricks that you will never get the better of me."

12. End — Thor goes back to Thrudvangur

When Thor had heard this speech he gripped his hammer and wielded it, but when he went to strike, he could not see Utgarda-Loki anywhere. And then he turned back to the fortress, intending to smash it up. He could see a beautiful rolling plain there, but no fortress. Then he turned back and went on his way until he came back to Thrudvangur. To tell the truth, he had decided then to try to arrange an encounter with the Midgard Serpent, which came about later.

I don't think anyone can give you a more truthful account of this journey of Thor's."